FOOTBALL maths

RED STRIP

DON SHAW & JOHN SHIELS

You are the manager

_____

Your team name

_____

Colour in your kit

Home kit   **Away kit**

OXFORD UNIVERSITY PRESS

How to use this book

The purpose of this series of fill-in workbooks is to give practice in Key Stage 2 Maths in a motivating context.

The contents list shows which topic of maths is covered on each page, which maths skill this comes under, and at what level. This will give you some indication of how your child might perform in the National Tests.

First of all, your child should decide on their team name, write it in on the title page, and colour their kit in home and away colours. On each page they can decide on a different opponent, and fill in their own team in the white box and the opposing team in the tinted box. The away games are always slightly harder than the home games. The cup featured is a European club competition and the teams chosen should reflect this.

There are three kinds of page, keyed in the top corner:

 League games, which cover exercises in number and data.

 Euro Cup games, which are all on shape and measures.

 Training sessions, which are just games for practice, and don't involve scoring.

To check your child's answers after each page, turn to the referee's decisions on page 30. Fill in your goals down the right-hand side of each page and your final score at the foot of the page. Then complete the grids below: for each league game you win, fill in 3 points, starting from the bottom of the table; for a draw, fill in just 1 point. For each cup game you win, fill in a box, starting from the bottom. If you draw 0–0, stage a replay.

 League

Champions		54 Points
Runners-up		51 Points
European place		48 Points
European place		45 Points
		42 Points
		39 Points
		36 Points
		33 Points
Mid		30 Points
		27 Points
Table		24 Points
		21 Points
		18 Points
		15 Points
		12 Points
Relegated		9 Points
Relegated		6 Points
Relegated		3 Points

 Euro Cup

	Final
	Semi-final
	Quarter-final
	3rd Round
	2nd Round
	1st Round

CONTENTS

Maths topic	Number & Algebra	Shape & Measures	Handling data	Page
Time sequencing	Level 3			**4–5**
Negative numbers	Level 3			**6**
Negative numbers	Level 3			**7**
Decimal notation	Level 3			**8**
Decimal notation	Level 3			**9**
Combinations			Level 3	**10**
Perimeters		Level 4		**11**
Pictograms			Level 3	**12**
Pictograms			Level 3	**13**
Co-ordinates			Level 3	**14**
Data handling			Level 3	**15**
Shapes		Level 4		**16**
Shapes		Level 4		**17**
Bar charts			Level 3	**18**
Bar charts			Level 3	**19**
Estimating measures		Level 4		**20**
Rounding numbers	Level 4			**21**
Adding money	Level 4			**22**
Area of shapes		Level 4		**23**
Multiplication	Level 3			**24**
Tessellations		Level 4		**25**
Fractions	Level 4			**26**
Time	Level 4			**27**
Co-ordinates			Level 4	**28**
Perimeters		Level 4		**29**

V

It's time to take the field for the new season!

United v City

Kick-off 7.30 p.m.

These events from an evening game have been mixed up.
Place them in order on the time-line opposite, and work out the
final score.

The first 2 have been done for you.

City score **8.00**	Full-time **9.15**	Leave home **6.00**	United score **9.00**
Kick-off **7.30**	Second half begins **8.30**	Leave ground **9.30**	Arrive home **10.15**
United score **7.45**	Arrive at ground **6.45**	Half-time **8.15**	Sit down **7.10**
City score **8.50**	United score **8.35**	Goal disallowed **7.46**	Goal disallowed **9.01**

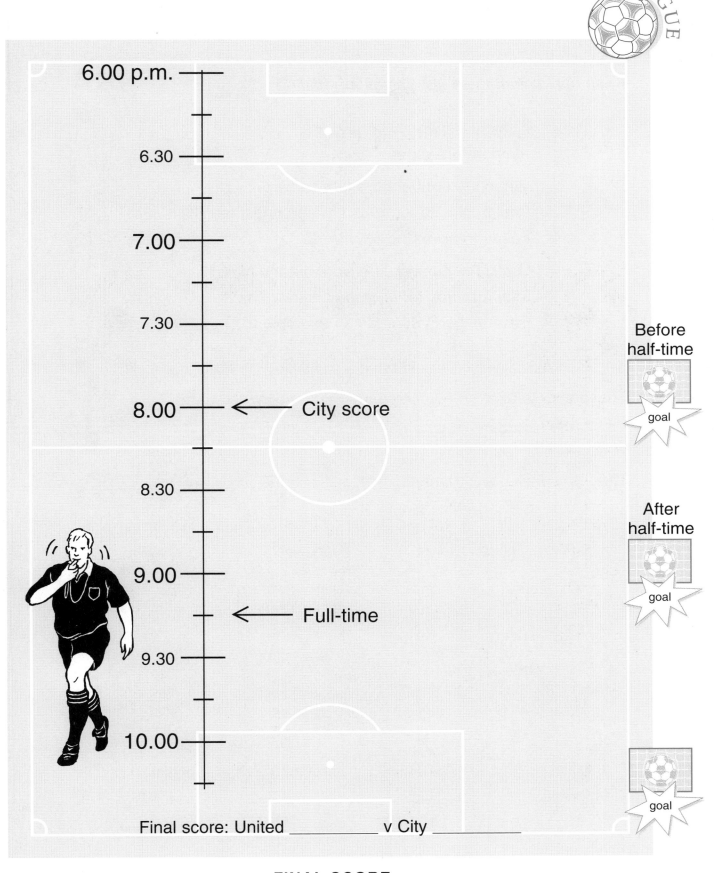

LEAGUE

6.00 p.m.

6.30

7.00

7.30

8.00 ← City score

8.30

9.00

← Full-time

9.30

10.00

Before half-time

goal

After half-time

goal

goal

Final score: United _____ v City _____

FINAL SCORE

| | | V | | 2 |

5

LEAGUE

Fill in your team names

V

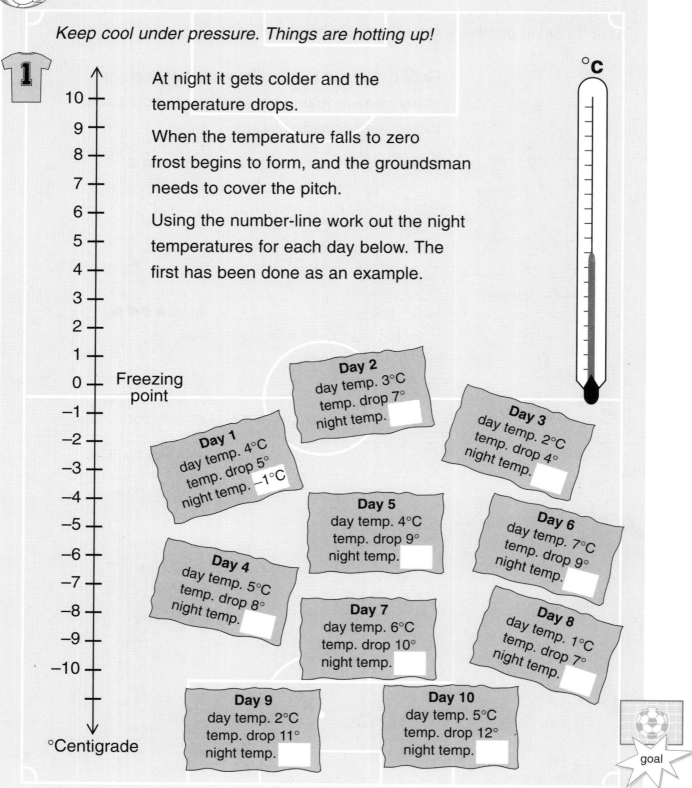

Keep cool under pressure. Things are hotting up!

°C

10
9
8
7
6
5
4
3
2
1
0 — Freezing point
−1
−2
−3
−4
−5
−6
−7
−8
−9
−10

°Centigrade

At night it gets colder and the temperature drops.

When the temperature falls to zero frost begins to form, and the groundsman needs to cover the pitch.

Using the number-line work out the night temperatures for each day below. The first has been done as an example.

Day 1
day temp. 4°C
temp. drop 5°
night temp. −1°C

Day 2
day temp. 3°C
temp. drop 7°
night temp. ☐

Day 3
day temp. 2°C
temp. drop 4°
night temp. ☐

Day 4
day temp. 5°C
temp. drop 8°
night temp. ☐

Day 5
day temp. 4°C
temp. drop 9°
night temp. ☐

Day 6
day temp. 7°C
temp. drop 9°
night temp. ☐

Day 7
day temp. 6°C
temp. drop 10°
night temp. ☐

Day 8
day temp. 1°C
temp. drop 7°
night temp. ☐

Day 9
day temp. 2°C
temp. drop 11°
night temp. ☐

Day 10
day temp. 5°C
temp. drop 12°
night temp. ☐

goal

FINAL SCORE

0 V

6

LEAGUE

Keep thinking positively – you can win this one!

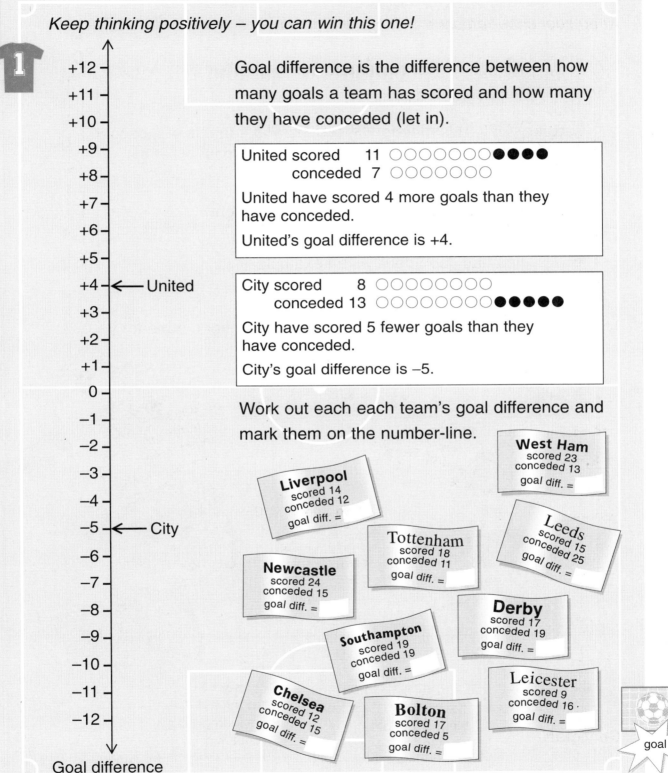

Goal difference is the difference between how many goals a team has scored and how many they have conceded (let in).

United scored   11 ○○○○○○○●●●●
     conceded 7 ○○○○○○○

United have scored 4 more goals than they have conceded.

United's goal difference is +4.

City scored   8 ○○○○○○○○
    conceded 13 ○○○○○○○○●●●●●

City have scored 5 fewer goals than they have conceded.

City's goal difference is –5.

Work out each each team's goal difference and mark them on the number-line.

West Ham
scored 23
conceded 13
goal diff. =

Liverpool
scored 14
conceded 12
goal diff. =

Leeds
scored 15
conceded 25
goal diff. =

Tottenham
scored 18
conceded 11
goal diff. =

Newcastle
scored 24
conceded 15
goal diff. =

Derby
scored 17
conceded 19
goal diff. =

Southampton
scored 19
conceded 19
goal diff. =

Leicester
scored 9
conceded 16
goal diff. =

Chelsea
scored 12
conceded 15
goal diff. =

Bolton
scored 17
conceded 5
goal diff. =

Number line labels: +12, +11, +10, +9, +8, +7, +6, +5, +4 ← United, +3, +2, +1, 0, –1, –2, –3, –4, –5 ← City, –6, –7, –8, –9, –10, –11, –12

Goal difference

goal

Fill in your team names

[   ] V [   ]

Time your runs from midfield to beat the offside and you're in on goal!

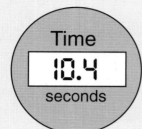

Time
10.4
seconds

The trainer times the players when they run 100 m.

Alan's time is 10.4 seconds.

This means 10 seconds and 4 tenths of a second.

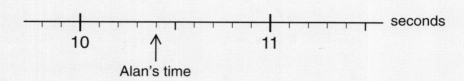

seconds

10   11

↑
Alan's time

1 Match these players with the arrows. The first has been done for you.

John	**Dave**	**Steve**	**Pete**
11.9 secs.	10.5 secs.	10.1 secs.	12.3 secs.

Howard	**Ryan**	**George**
11.4 secs.	10.9 secs.	12.8 secs.

seconds

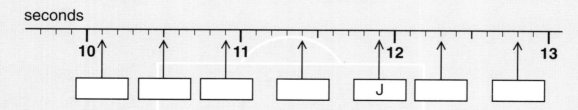

10↑   ↑   ↑**11**   ↑   ↑**12**   ↑   ↑**13**

[ ] [ ] [ ] [ ] [J] [ ] [ ]

goal

2 Who was the fastest? _____   Who was the slowest? _____

goal

FINAL SCORE

[   ] **1** V [   ]

	V	

Get numbers into the box and the chances will come!

1 These players are timed for a 400 m run.

Write down each player's time. The first has been done for you.

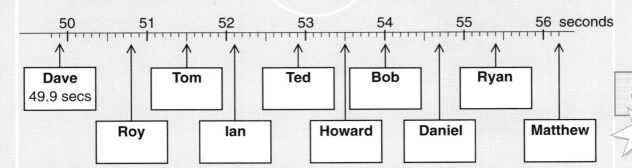

Dave 49.9 secs	Tom	Ted	Bob	Ryan

Roy	Ian	Howard	Daniel	Matthew

goal

2 Mark these players' transfer fees on the number-line.

The first has been done for you.

Smith
£6.2 million

Rogers
£7.5 million

Cope
£3.8 million

Day
£8.9 million

Edwards
£2.6 million

Chan
£10.3 million

Weir
£1.9 million

Bell
£4.7 million

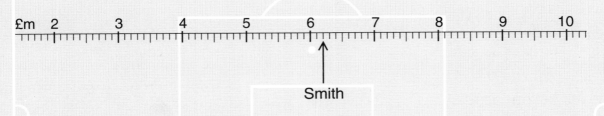

Smith

goal

FINAL SCORE

	V		1

Combine defence with counter attacks to beat this stylish team!

1 This team has 2 full kits.

If they mix up the shirts, shorts and socks they can make 8 different kits.

2 kits have been entered in the table below.

See if you can list the other 6 kits.

Shirt	Shorts	Socks
Green	Green	Green
Green	Green	White

goal

FINAL SCORE

0   V

FIRST ROUND

You're in Europe! You'll run rings round their defence!

The distance around the outside of a shape is called the perimeter.

Football pitches vary in size.

All pitches must be between 100 and 130 yards long and between 50 and 100 yards wide. (A yard is a little less than a metre.)

1 Work out the perimeters of these pitches.

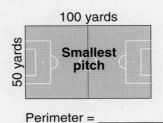

100 yards
50 yards
Smallest pitch

Perimeter = _____

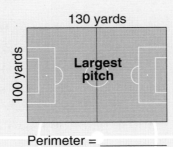

130 yards
100 yards
Largest pitch

Perimeter = _____

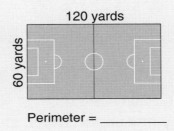

120 yards
60 yards

Perimeter = _____

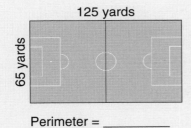

125 yards
65 yards

Perimeter = _____

104 yards
79 yards

Perimeter = _____

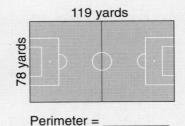

119 yards
78 yards

Perimeter = _____

2 Design a pitch that has a perimeter of 400 yards.

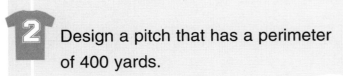

goal

3 A pitch is 110 yards long and has a perimeter of 350 yards.
How wide is it?

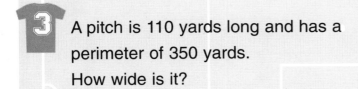

goal

LEAGUE

	V	

There's sure to be a big crowd. They're counting on you!

1

Team	Attendance
Newcastle	👤 👤 𝄻
Liverpool	👤 👤 👤 👤 👤
Tottenham	👤 👤 👤 𝄻
West Ham	👤 👤 👤 👤
Manchester	👤 👤 👤 👤 👤
Wimbledon	👤 𝄻

This pictogram shows the attendances at 6 grounds.

👤 = 10 000   𝄻 = 5000

(all figures rounded to nearest 5000)

Newcastle's attendance was   25 000

Liverpool's attendance was   _____

Tottenham's attendance was   _____

West Ham's attendance was   _____

Manchester's attendance was   _____

Wimbledon's attendance was   _____

goal

2

Players	Goals scored
Smith	◯ ◯ ◖
Barnes	◯ ◯ ◯ ◯ ◯ ◿
Dunn	◯ ◯ ◯ ◿
Key	◯ ◯ ◕
Bright	

This pictogram shows the goals scored by City's players in one season.
(Only even numbers of goals were scored.)

◯ = 8 goals   ◖ = 4 goals   ◿ = 2 goals   ◕ = 6 goals

Smith scored _____ goals

Barnes scored _____ goals

Dunn scored _____ goals

Key scored _____ goals

If Bright scored 14 goals complete the pictogram.

goal

FINAL SCORE

	V		1

LEAGUE

You can turn the tables on this fancied team if you try!

The number of goals scored by 7 teams last season were as follows:

Teams	Number of goals scored
Liverpool	40
Newcastle	80
Derby	50
Coventry	105
Blackburn	55
Wimbledon	30
Chelsea	75

Complete the pictogram below using ○ = 20 goals

◁ = 5 goals   ◖ = 10 goals   ◕ = 15 goals

(rounded to nearest 5 goals)

Teams	Number of goals scored
Liverpool	○ ○
Newcastle	
Derby	
Coventry	
Blackburn	
Wimbledon	
Chelsea	

goal

FINAL SCORE

Fill in your team names

[   ] V [   ]

You're a top team! Go out and prove it.

| Top 6 teams after 10 games | | | | | | | |
Team	P	W	D	L	F	A	Pts
West Ham	10	8	2	0	28	15	26
Tottenham	10	6	3	1	27	18	21
Leeds	10	5	4	1	29	10	19
Newcastle	10	6	0	4	17	8	18
Chelsea	10	5	3	2	16	21	18
Coventry	10	5	2	3	13	20	17

P   = games played

W   = games won

D   = games drawn

L   = games lost

F   = goals scored

A   = goals against

Pts = points

1 How many games have West Ham won? _____

How many games have Tottenham drawn? _____

How many games have Leeds lost? _____

2 How many games have Chelsea drawn? _____

How many goals have Coventry scored? _____

Which team has lost the most matches? _____

3 Which 2 teams have 18 points? _____

Which team has scored the most goals? _____

Which 2 teams have won 6 matches? _____

4 Which team has conceded the most goals? _____

Which 2 teams have drawn 2 matches? _____

Which 2 teams have lost 1 match? _____

FINAL SCORE

[   ] V [   ] **3**

LEAGUE

Everything points to a comfortable victory!

Teams are awarded 3 points for each win and 1 point for each draw.

1 Work out each team's points after 10 matches.

Liverpool
W	D	L	Pts
5	2	3	

Leicester
W	D	L	Pts
6	2	2	

Tottenham
W	D	L	Pts
3	6	1	

Newcastle
W	D	L	Pts
7	2	1	

West Ham
W	D	L	Pts
2	8	0	

Chelsea
W	D	L	Pts
4	1	5	

Blackburn
W	D	L	Pts
6	1	3	

Leeds
W	D	L	Pts
3	7	0	

goal

2 Now complete the league table for these 8 teams.

Top 8 teams after 10 games

	Team	Points
1	_____	_____
2	_____	_____
3	_____	_____
4	_____	_____
5	_____	_____
6	_____	_____
7	_____	_____
8	_____	_____

goal

CUP

Fill in your team names

[ ] V [ ]

SECOND ROUND

Match their style in midfield with your new diamond formation.

1 Join the names to the shapes.

kite   square   rhombus   rectangle   parallelogram

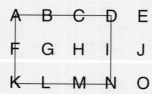

| 6 letters | 9 letters | 13 letters | 7 letters | 4 letters |

goal

2 In training the manager marks letters on the ground and the players have to run between them.

John is told to run A → D → N → K → A.

```
A  B  C  D  E
F  G  H  I  J
K  L  M  N  O
P  Q  R  S  T
```

John's run made a rectangle.

Mark these runs on the letters and say what shapes they have made.

Pete runs B → E → T → Q → B.

```
A  B  C  D  E
F  G  H  I  J
K  L  M  N  O
P  Q  R  S  T
U  V  W  X  Y
```

Pete's run makes

a _____ .

Ryan runs F → J → T → P → F.

```
A  B  C  D  E
F  G  H  I  J
K  L  M  N  O
P  Q  R  S  T
U  V  W  X  Y
```

Ryan's run makes

a _____ .

goal

FINAL SCORE

[ ] V [ ] **1**

16

V

THIRD ROUND

Shape up for this next big European challenge!

1

Carl runs C → N → W → L → C.

A B C D E
F G H I J
K L M N O
P Q R S T
U V W X Y

Carl's run makes

a _____ .

Dave runs G → J → S → P → G.

A B C D E
F G H I J
K L M N O
P Q R S T
U V W X Y

Dave's run makes

a _____ .

Mike runs C → O → W → K → C.

A B C D E
F G H I J
K L M N O
P Q R S T
U V W X Y

Mike's run makes

a _____ .

Denis runs F → C → J → W → F.

A B C D E
F G H I J
K L M N O
P Q R S T
U V W X Y

Denis's run makes

a _____ .

Steve runs U → G → E → S → U.

A B C D E
F G H I J
K L M N O
P Q R S T
U V W X Y

Steve's run makes

a _____ .

Phil runs V → P → D → J → V.

A B C D E
F G H I J
K L M N O
P Q R S T
U V W X Y

Phil's run makes

a _____ .

goal

FINAL SCORE

0   V

17

[ ] **V** [ ]

This will be a good chance to chart your progress this season!

1 Dave keeps a tally count of the goals scored by United's players during a season.

Add up the tally marks to complete the table.

Players	Tally	Number of goals scored
Evans	III	3
Lee	ℍ II	7
Hall	ℍ ℍ I	
Burns	ℍ ℍ ℍ ℍ I	
Thomas	ℍ IIII	
Dean	ℍ ℍ II	
Kay	IIII	

goal

2 Complete the bar chart to show the goals scored by United's players.

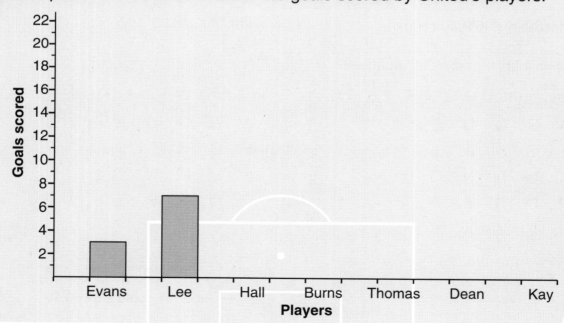

goal

FINAL SCORE

[ ] **1** **V** [ ]

Their marking is poor – you can get amongst the goals!

1 Dave keeps a record of United's results.

Complete the tally chart.

Results	Tally	Number of games
Won	ЖЖ ЖЖ ЖЖ II	17
Drawn	ЖЖ IIII	
Lost	ЖЖ ЖЖ III	

2 Complete the bar chart showing United's results.

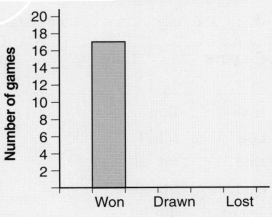

goal

goal

3 Dave keeps a record of the number of goals scored each game.

1	2	1	2	1	0	1	3	1	1	1	2	2	0	1		
2	2	0	1	5	3	1	2	1	0	4	1	2	1	0		
0	2	3	1	3	2	0	1	4	1	3	0	2	4	3		

Complete the tally chart.

Number of goals scored	Tally	Number of games
0		
1		
2		
3		
4		
5		

4 Draw a bar chart to show this information.

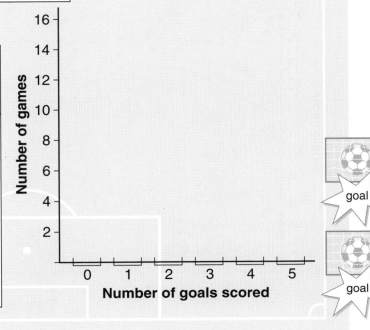

goal

goal

goal

FINAL SCORE

V   2

19

[ ] **V** [ ]

QUARTER-FINAL

I reckon you'll measure up to this challenge and go all the way!

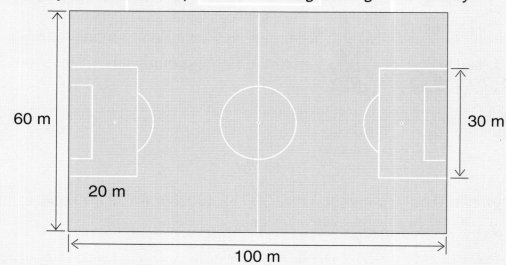

60 m   30 m

20 m

100 m

1 Using the measurements on the diagram above, try to estimate the distances marked on the diagrams below.

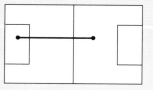

_____

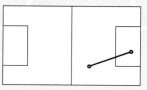

_____

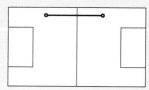

_____

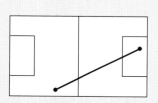

_____

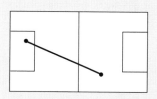

_____

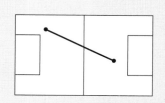

_____

goal

2 Lee passes the ball 55 m. Draw an estimate of this pass on this diagram.

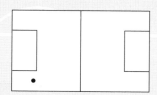

goal

FINAL SCORE

[ ] **V** [ ] **1**

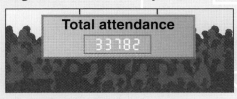

V

A great chance for you to round up all three points!

Total attendance

33782

Big numbers are often rounded off to the nearest thousand.

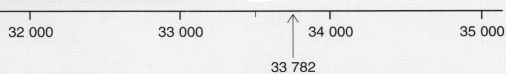

32 000   33 000   34 000   35 000

33 782

On the number-line you can see that 33 782 is between 33 000 and 34 000 but it is nearer to 34 000.

We say that 33 782 rounded to the nearest thousand is 34 000.

> The rule for rounding is if the number ends in 500 or more then it rounds up to the next thousand. If the number ends in less than 500 then it rounds down.

Round off these attendances to the nearest thousand.

1

Coventry v Sheffield	**Liverpool v Leeds**	**Tottenham v Villa**
Attendance **22 649**	Attendance **43 298**	Attendance **31 746**
_____ to nearest thousand	_____ to nearest thousand	_____ to nearest thousand

goal

2

Wimbledon v Coventry	**Palace v Derby**	**West Ham v Barnsley**
Attendance **14 864**	Attendance **17 681**	Attendance **23 298**
_____ to nearest thousand	_____ to nearest thousand	_____ to nearest thousand

goal

3

Southampton v Everton	**Blackburn v Bolton**	**Manchester v Chelsea**
Attendance **18 145**	Attendance **16 564**	Attendance **49 298**
_____ to nearest thousand	_____ to nearest thousand	_____ to nearest thousand

goal

FINAL SCORE

2   V

Fill in your team names

[ ] V [ ]

This is adding up to a great season spent in the highest company!

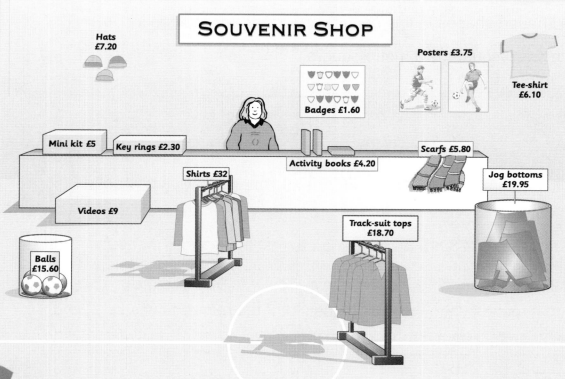

SOUVENIR SHOP

Hats £7.20

Badges £1.60

Posters £3.75

Tee-shirt £6.10

Mini kit £5

Key rings £2.30

Activity books £4.20

Scarfs £5.80

Shirts £32

Jog bottoms £19.95

Videos £9

Track-suit tops £18.70

Balls £15.60

1 Work out how much these people spend.

Ball	
Tee-shirt	
Total	

Dave

Track-suit top	
Hat	
Total	

Chloe

Ball	
Scarf	
Total	

James

Poster	
Badge	
Total	

Karen

Jog bottoms	
Scarf	
Total	

Kate

Track-suit top	
Jog bottoms	
Total	

Tom

goal

FINAL SCORE

[ ] V [ ] **0**

V

SEMI-FINAL

The team may be on the spot. Concentrate in all areas of the field!

The shaded shapes in this penalty area need reseeding.

Each small square is a metre square. ☐ = 1 m²

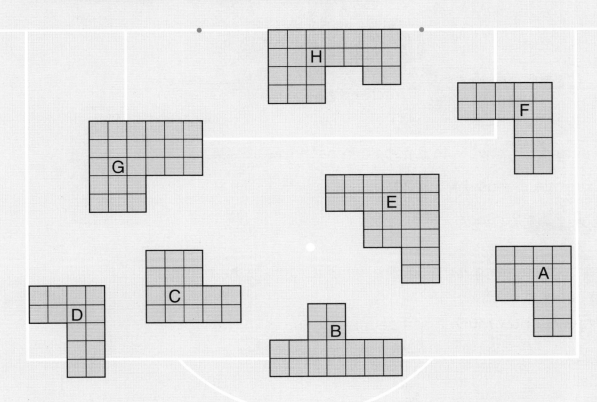

Work out the area of each shaded shape by counting the squares inside it.

Area of Ⓐ = _____   Area of Ⓑ = _____

Area of Ⓒ = _____   Area of Ⓓ = _____

Area of Ⓔ = _____   Area of Ⓕ = _____

Area of Ⓖ = _____   Area of Ⓗ = _____

FINAL SCORE

V   1

	V	

The problems seem to be multiplying, so don't count on this being easy!

Without counting each one, can you work out how many people there are in this box?

Directors' Box

There are 4 rows with 5 people in each row.

We write this as $4 \times 5 = 20$

There are 20 people altogether.

1 Without counting each square, write a sum for the number of seats in each box below.

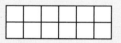

_____ × _____ = _____

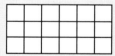

_____ × _____ = _____

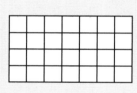

_____ × _____ = _____

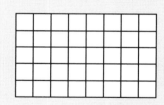

_____ × _____ = _____

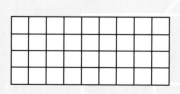

_____ × _____ = _____

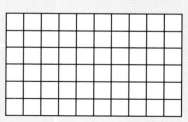

_____ × _____ = _____

goal

FINAL SCORE

	0	V		

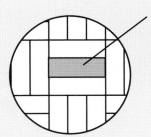

This ball is made from rectangles stitched together.

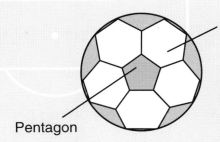

Hexagon

Pentagon

This ball is made from pentagons and hexagons stitched together.

If shapes fit together without leaving any gaps we say that the shapes tessellate.

Liverpool are tiling a wall with L-shaped tiles.

Add 10 more tiles to the wall to keep the pattern going.

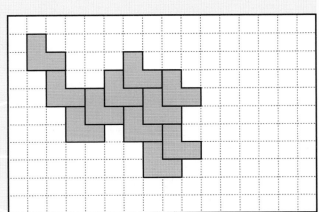

Tottenham are tiling a wall with T-shaped tiles.

Add 10 more tiles to the wall to keep the pattern going.

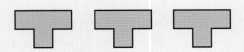

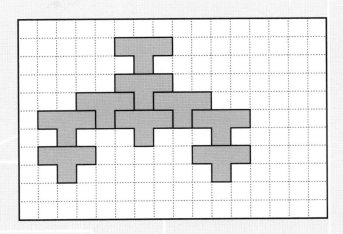

Fill in your team names

V

You've only a fraction of your normal away support. Play as a unit!

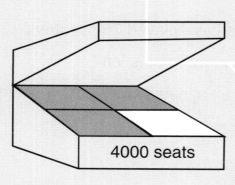

This stand is $\frac{3}{4}$ full.

How many people are there in this stand?

We need to work out $\frac{3}{4}$ of 4000

$\frac{1}{4}$ of 4000 is 1000

then $\frac{3}{4}$ of 4000 is 3 times 1000.

There are 3000 people in this stand.

1 Work out how many people there are in each of these stands.

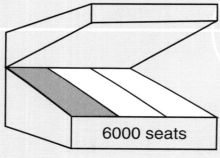

6000 seats

$\frac{1}{3}$ of 6000 = _____

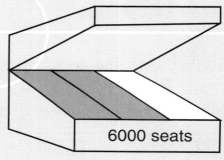

6000 seats

$\frac{2}{3}$ of 6000 = _____

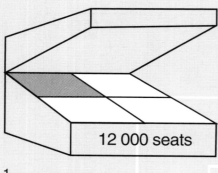

12 000 seats

$\frac{1}{4}$ of 12 000 = _____

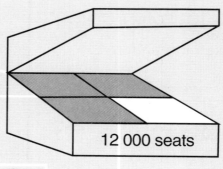

12 000 seats

$\frac{3}{4}$ of 12 000 = _____

FINAL SCORE

2 V

26

Time's running out this season – keep going right to the end!

If the teams have played 78 minutes 12 seconds, how long is left?

A match is 90 minutes long.

mins.

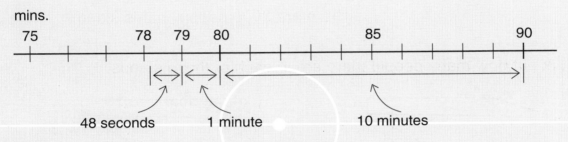

48 seconds   1 minute   10 minutes

There are 11 minutes and 48 seconds left.

Work out how long is left in these matches.

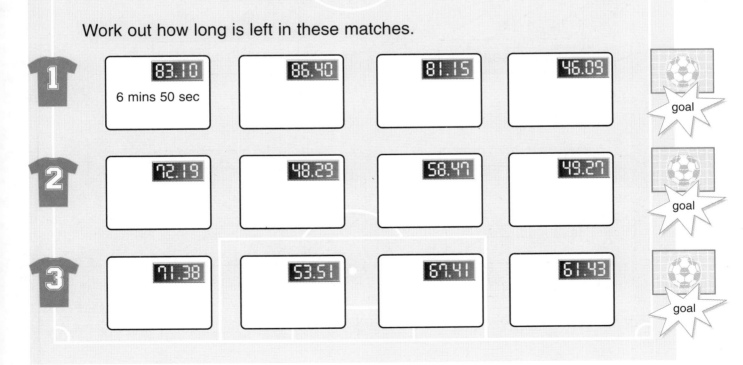

FINAL SCORE

V

Can you pass this test and end the season in triumph!

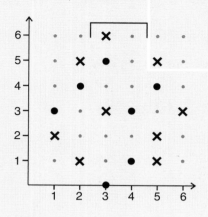

Starting at the point (3,0) pass the ball to members of your team ● making sure that you avoid the defenders ✕.

There are many possible answers and one of them is written below.

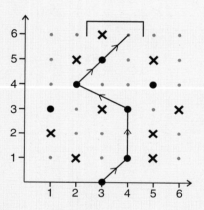

Route to goal

Start   **Goal**

(3,0) → (4,1) → (4,3) → (2,4) → (3,5) → (4,6)

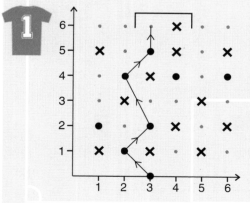

Write down this route to goal.

Start   **Goal**

(3,0) → (   ) → (   ) → (   ) → (   ) → (   )

goal

FINAL SCORE

V   **0**

V

THE FINAL

You've reached the Euro Cup Final! Enjoy your lap of honour.

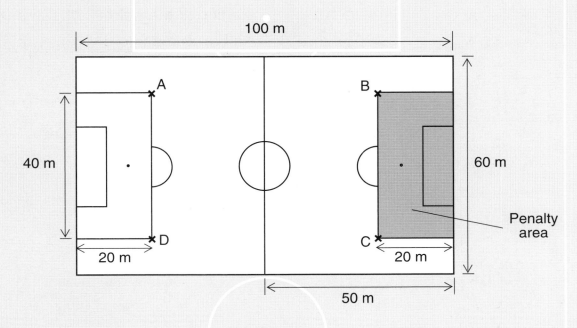

1 What is the distance around the pitch? _____

If you take one half of the pitch, what is the distance around it? _____

What is the distance around the penalty area? _____

2 How far is 2 complete laps of the pitch? _____

How far is 6 complete laps of the pitch? _____

Steve wants to run 1000 m. How many full laps must he run? _____

3 John runs twice around half the pitch and Dave runs once around the whole pitch. How much further does John run? _____

Ryan runs from cone A to cone B. How far does he run? _____

Pete runs between cones A, B, C and D. How far does he run? _____

FINAL SCORE

V   **2**

29

ANSWERS

The referee's decision is final!

▶ PAGES **4** and **5**

1 **Before half-time**
6.00, 6.45, 7.10, 7.30, 7.45, 7.46, 8.00, 8.15

Five or more correct answers scores a goal.

After half-time
8.30, 8.35, 8.50, 9.00, 9.01, 9.15, 9.30, 10.15

Five or more correct answers scores a goal.

United 1, City 2

Correct score, scores a goal

▶ PAGE **6**

1 2 = –4°C, 3 = –2°C, 4 = –3°C,
5 = –5°C, 6 = –2°C, 7 = –4°C,
8 = –6°C, 9 = –9°C, 10 = –7°C

Six or more correct answers scores a goal.

▶ PAGE **7**

1 Liverpool +2, Tottenham +7,
West Ham +10, Newcastle +9,
Leeds –10, Southampton 0,
Derby –2, Chelsea –3, Bolton +12,
Leicester –7

Four or more correct answers scores a goal.
Seven or more correct answers scores two goals.

▶ PAGE **8**

1

Four or more correct answers scores a goal.

2 Steve was the fastest
George was the slowest

Both correct to score a goal.

▶ PAGE **9**

1 Roy 50.8, Tom 51.5, Ian 52.1,
Ted 52.9, Howard 53.5, Bob 54.0,
Daniel 54.7, Ryan 55.4, Matthew 56.2

Six or more correct answers scores a goal.

2

Four or more correct answers scores a goal.

▶ PAGE **10**

1

Shirt	Shorts	Socks
Green	White	Green
Green	White	White
White	White	White
White	White	Green
White	Green	White
White	Green	Green

Four or more correct answers scores a goal.

▶ PAGE **11**

1
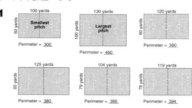

Four or more answers within 5 metres scores a goal.

2 Many possible correct answers

3 65 yards wide

▶ PAGE **12**

1 Liverpool 50 000, Tottenham = 35 000,
West Ham = 30 000, Manchester
60 000, Wimbledon 15 000

Three or more correct answers scores a goal.

2 Smith 20, Barnes 42, Dunn 34,
Key 22, Bright ◯ ◔

Three or more correct answers scores a goal.

▶ PAGE **13**

1

Teams	Number of goals scored
Newcastle	◯ ◯ ◯ ◯
Derby	◯ ◯ ◖
Coventry	◯ ◯ ◯ ◯ ◯ ◹
Blackburn	◯ ◯ ◕
Wimbledon	◯ ◖
Chelsea	◯ ◯ ◗ ◕

Four or more correct answers scores a goal.

▶ PAGE **14**

1 8, 3, 1

Two or more correct answers scores a goal.

2 3, 13, Newcastle

Two or more correct answers scores a goal.

3 Newcastle and Chelsea, Leeds,
Tottenham and Newcastle

Two or more correct answers scores a goal.

4 Chelsea, West Ham and Coventry,
Tottenham and Leeds

Two or more correct answers scores a goal.

▶ PAGE **15**

1 Liverpool 17, Leicester 20,
Tottenham 15, Newcastle 23,
West Ham 14, Chelsea 13,
Blackburn 19, Leeds 16

Five or more correct answers scores a goal.

2

Top 8 teams after 10 games		
	Team	Points
1	Newcastle	23
2	Leicester	20
3	Blackburn	19
4	Liverpool	17
5	Leeds	16
6	Tottenham	15
7	West Ham	14
8	Chelsea	13

Five or more correct answers scores a goal.

▶ PAGE **16**

1

Three or more correct answers scores a goal.

2 Pete's run makes a square
Ryan's run makes a rectangle

Both correct answers scores a goal.

▶ PAGE **17**

1 Carl's run makes a rhombus
Dave's run makes a parallelogram
Mike's run makes a square
Denis's run makes a kite
Steve's run makes a rhombus
Phil's run makes a rectangle

Four or more correct answers scores a goal.

▶ PAGE **18**

1 Hall 11, Burns 21, Thomas 9, Dean 12, Kay 4

Three or more correct answers scores a goal.

2
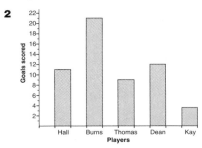

Three or more correct answers scores a goal.

▶ PAGE **19**

1

Results	Tally	Number of games
Drawn	Ⅲ IIII	9
Lost	Ⅲ ⅢI III	13

Both correct answers scores a goal.

2
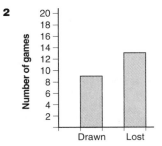

Both correct answers scores a goal.

3

Number of goals scored	Tally	Number of games
0	ⅢI III	8
1	ⅢI ⅢI ⅢI I	16
2	ⅢI ⅢI I	11
3	ⅢI I	6
4	III	3
5	I	1

Four or more correct answers scores a goal.

4
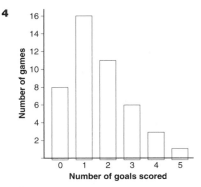

Four or more correct answers scores a goal.

▶ PAGE **20**

1
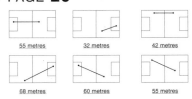

Four or more correct answers within 5 metres scores a goal.

2 Draw a line 20 mm in length.

▶ PAGE **21**

1 23 000, 43 000, 32 000

Two or more correct answers scores a goal.

2 15 000, 18 000, 23 000

Two or more correct answers scores a goal.

3 18 000, 17 000, 49 000

Two or more correct answers scores a goal.

▶ PAGE **22**

1 Dave – £15.60 + £6.10 = £21.70
Chloe – £18.70 + £7.20 = £25.90
James – £15.60 + £5.80 = £21.40
Karen – £3.75 + £1.60 = £5.35
Kate – £19.95 + £5.80 = £25.75
Tom – £18.70 + £19.95 = £38.65

Four or more correct answers scores a goal.

▶ PAGE **23**

1 A = 16 m², B = 18 m²,
C = 16 m², D = 14 m²

Three or more correct answers scores a goal.

2 E = 24 m², F = 16 m²,
G = 24 m², H = 22 m²

Three or more correct answers scores a goal.

▶ PAGE **24**

1 6 × 2 = 12   6 × 3 = 18
7 × 4 = 28   8 × 5 = 40
9 × 4 = 36   10 × 6 = 60

Four or more correct answers scores a goal.

▶ PAGE **26**

1 2000   4000
3000   9000

Each correct answer scores a goal.

▶ PAGE **27**

1 3 mins 20 secs, 8 mins 45 secs,
43 mins 51 secs

Two or more correct answers scores a goal.

2 17 mins 41 secs, 41 mins 31 secs,
31 mins 13 secs, 40 mins 33 secs

Three or more correct answers scores a goal.

3 18 mins 22 secs, 36 mins 9 secs,
22 mins 19 secs, 28 mins 17 secs

Three or more correct answers scores a goal.

▶ PAGE **28**

1 (2,1) → (3,2) → (2,4) → (3,5) → (3,6)

Three or more correct answers scores a goal.

▶ PAGE **29**

1 320 metres, 220 metres, 120 metres

Two or more correct answers scores a goal.

2 640 metres, 1920 metres, 4 full laps

Two or more correct answers scores a goal.

3 120 metres, 60 metres, 160 metres

Two or more correct answers scores a goal.

Bobby Charlton Soccer Schools

'Learning through Football' Special School courses are available at the Bobby Charlton Soccer School HQ in Manchester throughout the year, either residentially or non residential. All participants will be able to tackle the problems of Key Stage 2 Maths and English, as well as receive expert tuition putting them through their soccer paces. There will also be an opportunity to visit the great Manchester attractions of Manchester United FC and Granada Tours. For further details contact John Shiels at Bobby Charlton Sports School, Hopwood Hall, Rochdale Road, Middleton, Manchester, M24 6XH or Telephone: 0161 643 3113 Fax: 0161 643 1444.

Individual courses in Maths and football are available each Easter vacation.

Oxford University Press, Great Clarendon Street, Oxford OX2 6DP

Oxford New York

*Athens Auckland Bangkok Bogota Bombay Buenos Aires
Calcutta Cape Town Dar es Salaam Delhi
Florence Hong Kong Istanbul Karachi
Kuala Lumpur Madras Madrid Melbourne
Mexico City Nairobi Paris Singapore
Taipei Tokyo Toronto Warsaw*

*and associated companies in
Berlin Ibadan*

Oxford is a trade mark of Oxford University Press

© Oxford University Press 1998
First published 1998
Reprinted 1999

ISBN 019 838225 1

Typeset and designed by Oxford Designers & Illustrators, Oxford

Printed in Hong Kong